JUL   2013

DISCARD
FCPL discards materials
that are outdated and in poor condition.
In order to make room for current,
in-demand materials, underused materials
are offered for public sale.

TIPS FOR
SUCCESS

TOP 10 TIPS

FOR DEVELOPING MONEY MANAGEMENT SKILLS

LARRY GERBER

ROSEN
PUBLISHING

NEW YORK

Published in 2013 by The Rosen Publishing Group, Inc.
29 East 21st Street, New York, NY 10010

Copyright © 2013 by The Rosen Publishing Group, Inc.

First Edition

All rights reserved. No part of this book may be reproduced in any form without permission in writing from the publisher, except by a reviewer.

Library of Congress Cataloging-in-Publication Data

Gerber, Larry, 1946–
Top 10 tips for developing money management skills/Larry Gerber. — 1st ed.
    p. cm. — (Tips for success)
Includes bibliographical references and index.
ISBN 978-1-4488-6862-9 (library binding)
1. Finance, Personal—Juvenile literature. I. Title. II. Title: Top ten tips for developing money management skills.
HG179.G455 2013
332.024—dc23

2011052048

Manufactured in the United States of America

CPSIA Compliance Information: Batch #S12YA: For further information, contact Rosen Publishing, New York, New York, at 1-800-237-9932.

CONTENTS

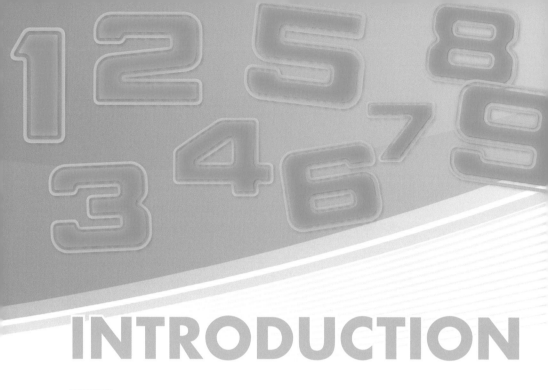

INTRODUCTION

Some people never seem to have money problems. They may not be rich, but they usually have enough to buy the things they need and do the things they want to do. Even when they're short of cash, these fortunate folks don't seem to worry too much about it. It's as if they know a payday is coming—and often it is. When it comes to money, they seem to have the magic touch.

Many of us experience the magic of money in another way— by watching it vanish without a trace. We often have a hard time getting the things we really need, let alone the things we want. Some people borrow and have a hard time repaying. They tend to be stressed out a lot, and it's easy to see why. Are they just unlucky, or what?

It's no wonder that money is the cause of so many disagreements. Sometimes it appears to be some kind of evil force. At other times, however, it seems like money really could buy

happiness, if we just had enough of it. In this book, we'll try to think about money more as a tool—sort of like a Swiss Army knife that we can use for a lot of different tasks and to help create the things we want in our lives.

Money really is like a tool, in more ways than one. It's an all-purpose survival kit because without it, life gets really tough really fast. It's so handy we always want to keep it around. If we handle money carelessly, however, it can turn on us and do serious damage. And just like any tool, sometimes it works great,

Money means different things to different people, and it sometimes seems more powerful than it really is. Thinking of money as a tool helps keep it in perspective.

and sometimes it doesn't, depending on how skillfully it is utilized and operated.

These ten tips are ideas shared by lots of people, from billionaires to working-class moms, dads, and kids. Some tips are about doing specific things: writing, adding, and subtracting. Others suggest ways of thinking more carefully and deliberately about money and what we choose to do with it. One or two of the tips call for some honest thinking about ourselves and our priorities.

All of the tips are intended to help readers get the most out of this tool we call money, whether we're dealing with a lot of it or only a little. The end goal is not so much gaining as much money as possible as it is managing your financial resources to achieve life-long security, comfort, and happiness. Most of the ideas behind each tip are pretty basic. When it comes to handling money, ten tips are just a starting point. Like any other skill, managing money takes practice.

SET FINANCIAL GOALS

Many people who do well with money have something in common: they know what they want. Their goals may be long-term dreams like "I want to be able to support a family," or "I want to be able to retire early and travel the world." Or they may be short-term desires: "I need something cool to wear to the concert next month." When you set goals, you're initiating a very important process: you're starting to take responsibility for your own finances.

TAKING RESPONSIBILITY

Responsibility for money? That may sound strange to young people who legally require permission from their parents to open a bank account, use a credit card, or take a job. How can you take responsibility for something that you aren't even allowed to control yet?

CAN YOU SIMPLY DECIDE TO BE RICH?

When wealthy people explain how they made their millions, many of them say they set one financial goal early on. It's not a worksheet-type goal as much as a state of mind. Quite simply, they just decided to be rich and achieve "financial independence" or "financial freedom." "After my decision to get rich, I began taking action," writes Larry Winget, author of the book *You're Broke Because You Want to Be.* "I got a picture in my mind what rich looked like, felt like, and smelled like. I started writing things down. I made lists with details of how I wanted to live and what I wanted to have." Making a commitment is one way to focus our thinking, and our thoughts guide our actions.

Sooner or later, you'll get your hands on some cash of your own—gifts, allowance, odd-job money, or a paycheck from an after-school job—along with the ability to choose what to do with it. Let's say you get several birthday checks totaling $500. Looking around at all the stuff $500 will buy, it seems like there are dozens, even hundreds of possible spending choices.

Let's back up for a second, however. When it comes to basic decisions about what to do with money, there are really only a few. You can spend it now. You can save or invest it. You can spend some now while also saving or investing some. You can give it away by donating to a charity or loaning it to somebody. What's the responsible choice, especially in terms of your financial goals?

Financial responsibility means using money in a productive way that's in your own best interests or those of your family.

It usually means looking beyond the things you want today and instead thinking about the things you're going to need in the future.

HOW GOAL-SETTING WORKS

For example, let's say you know for sure that you're going to need a new laptop. One you realize that, it's time to start planning. Take a paper and pencil, and divide a page into four columns. In the left column, write down exactly what you want. Be specific. If you haven't decided on a laptop model, do the research, compare prices, and choose. We'll pretend that the goal is the latest Mac laptop. Write it down.

Now go to the next column on the right and put down how much it costs. Let's say you've decided on the model that's listed

Budget worksheets can be downloaded or drawn up with a paper and pencil. Whether they are fancy or informal, budgets are a major financial planning tool.

9

at $1,499. Don't forget to add taxes and any extras, like a maintenance guarantee.

In the third column, write down the date you want to buy the item. We'll say that you need the computer to start school on September 1. How many weeks or months away is that date? Divide the cost of the item by the number of weeks or months, and you'll see how much you have to save each week or month in order to get the computer. This number goes in column four on the right.

This exercise doesn't tell you how you're going to get the money, but it does help you keep in mind what you want, how much money is needed, and how much must be saved each week or month to reach the goal. Writing down specific financial goals will keep you focused on the target and make it more likely that you'll hit it. It also provides a way to keep track of progress. The same method works for short-term or long-term goals. This could include anything from a weekend dinner and movie date or a school trip four weeks from now to a car, college tuition, and apartment costs in four years.

And that $500 birthday money? If you put some or all of it into the laptop fund, your target is going to be that much closer. You're already one-third of the way toward the purchase price. Many Web sites offer free worksheets and other tools to help with savings targets and other financial planning goals. Many include calculators for the math-challenged. Just use the search term "setting financial goals" and see what the search engine comes up with.

MYTHS & FACTS

MYTH: YOU HAVE TO BE GOOD AT MATH TO BE SUCCESSFUL WITH MONEY.

FACT: SOME PEOPLE WITHOUT ADVANCED MATH SKILLS ARE NEVERTHELESS VERY SKILLED AT MONEY MANAGEMENT, JUST AS SOME PEOPLE HAVE A NATURAL TALENT FOR SPORTS, GAMES, LANGUAGES, OR SCIENCE. TO MANAGE MONEY, YOU DO NEED BASIC ARITHMETIC, BUT YOU DON'T HAVE TO BE A MATH GENIUS.

MYTH: YOU ARE WHAT YOU HAVE.

FACT: POSSESSIONS DON'T DEFINE PEOPLE. IT'S TRUE THAT SOME PEOPLE SEE THEIR POSSESSIONS AS EXTENSIONS OF THEMSELVES, AND THEY MAY TRY TO DEFINE THEMSELVES BY WHAT THEY HAVE. HOWEVER, PSYCHOLOGISTS SAY PEOPLE WHO THINK THIS WAY MAY JUST BE INSECURE. THEY'RE UNCERTAIN ABOUT THEIR OWN IDENTITIES SO THEY USE MATERIAL GOODS AND OBJECTS TO DEFINE OR EXTERIOR-IZE THEIR INNER SELVES.

MYTH: RICHES AND FAME GO HAND-IN-HAND.

FACT: SOMETIMES THEY DO; SOMETIMES THEY DON'T. AT THE TIME OF HIS DEATH, MICHAEL JACKSON WAS REPORTED TO BE $400 MILLION IN DEBT. ACTRESS KIM BASINGER, RAPPER MC HAMMER, AND BOXING CHAMP MIKE TYSON HAVE ALL DECLARED BANKRUPTCY. ON THE OTHER HAND, HOW FAMOUS ARE THOMAS SECUNDA, MURAT ULKER, AND MARTIN NAUGHTON? YOU'VE PROBABLY NEVER HEARD OF THEM, BUT THEY'RE ALL BILLIONAIRES.

TIP #2

MAKE MORE THAN YOU SPEND

If there were only one tip to remember, it would be this: make more than you spend. Or, to put it another way, never spend more than you make. Many experts call it the key to financial success. In many ways, it IS financial success. "Make more than you spend" is one of those old sayings that is so simple that it seems obvious. Simple and obvious are not the same thing as easy, however.

ADJUSTING SPENDING LEVELS

No matter what kind of job or how big an allowance you have, you can't always control your income. It may increase and decrease, and there's not always much you can do about it. But you can control your spending. When income drops, so, too, should spending. And when it rises again, spending can increase as well, but consider laying some of the extra money aside as a hedge against the next income downturn. Spending must be carefully monitored, controlled, and adjusted if you are to stay on the plus side of the income vs. expenditure balance.

INCOME VS. EXPENDITURE

In this context, the word "make" in the expression "make more than you spend" means earning or otherwise acquiring (through gifts or investments, for example) money over a period of time. This is income. The opposite of income is expenditure, or what we spend. When income is greater than or equal to expenditure, we are said to be living within our means. When income is less than expenditure, we're in debt. The income vs. expenditure balance can mean the difference between comfort and misery.

Generating and increasing income can be tough. Many experts recommend that parents give their kids allowances that increase as they get older so they can learn to save and keep track of their money. But an allowance often isn't enough to meet a teen's spending wants and needs, even when parents are generous. The answer, of course, is to seek out a paying job.

EMPLOYMENT

Finding a job—especially one that pays regularly—is often challenging in and of itself. In the United States, the minimum work age for most companies or businesses is fourteen. However, there are exceptions, such as employment at farms, family businesses, and in the entertainment industry. Working hours are limited, too: three hours a day during the school year, eight hours a day in summer. Underage workers seldom get the official minimum wage. They often need to get working papers and always need the consent of a parent or guardian. Regulations vary from place to place, and school counselors usually can provide you with your state and local employment regulations.

Pet care, yard work, and babysitting are widely available student jobs, but they're not the only ones. Many kids find ways to make money using their unique talents or skills.

These minimum age laws weren't passed to keep kids from making money, but to end the abusive and often cruel child labor practices that were common in the nineteenth and early decades of the twentieth centuries. These regulations do not prevent young people from entrepreneurial self-employment and the starting and operating of their own businesses and money-making schemes.

Lawn mowing, babysitting, dog walking, and cleaning chores are common jobs for self-employed students. Sometimes it might seem like they are the ONLY jobs available to young people. Research and creative thinking, however, can lead to dozens of employment and money-making possibilities. It helps to start by asking yourself a couple of questions: "What kind of work would I like to do?" and "What am I good at?"

TIP #3

SAVE, SAVE, SAVE!

Young people may be at a disadvantage when it comes to generating income, but they have a definite advantage when it comes to saving their money. The sooner in life a person starts saving, the more time he or she has for the savings to grow. Setting aside just a small amount each week or month can result in a substantial store of cash before long. For example, if you set aside just $5 a week, you will have saved $260 in a year.

Money deposited in savings accounts usually earns compound interest. The percentage may not be much, but the amount is constantly growing, and the money isn't at risk.

SAFETY AND SECURITY

There are two important questions to consider when you start saving. First: "Is my money safe?" Obviously, you don't want your money to get lost or stolen, but "keeping it safe" also means keeping it safe from yourself. If the savings are stashed at home in a piggy bank, it's easy to take some whenever there's a temptation to spend it. If the money is instead deposited in a bank or credit union, necessary withdrawals can still be fast and easy. But at least you have to go through a process that will slow you down enough to allow thought, deliberation, and reconsideration of the spending impulse. There's more time to think about whether the withdrawal is really necessary and worth it.

BEATING INFLATION AND EARNING INTEREST

The second question to ask yourself is "Will my savings keep up with inflation?" Over time, the prices of most things generally go up. Rarely do they go down, and not for long. This constant rise in the price of goods and services is known as inflation.

One way to combat the rising prices of inflation (and the consequent decrease in the purchasing power of each dollar) is by earning interest on your savings and investments. In financial terms, interest is a fee that's paid for the use of money. When we put money into a savings account, the bank or credit union pays us interest because it gets to use the money until we take it out.

HIGHER-INTEREST SAVINGS

Certificates of deposit, or CDs, are basically agreements between a bank or credit union and a customer. The customer agrees to leave his or her money in an account for the period of the CD—usually from six months to up to five years. The bank pays a higher interest rate to the depositor than it does on its regular savings accounts. Most CDs require an initial deposit of at least $500. Money market accounts also pay higher interest than savings accounts. They also require a minimum deposit, usually, $1,000 or more, and limit the withdrawals you can make.

U.S. government bonds are similar to CDs, but they are guaranteed by the government and designed to stay even with the inflation rate. The least expensive savings bonds cost only $25. Government bonds are sold online through the U.S. Department of Treasury at www .treasurydirect.gov.

Compound interest can help grow your savings without any effort on your part. Here's how compounding works: Let's say you put money into a savings account that pays monthly interest. After one month, the interest is calculated on the original deposit, which is called the principal, and it's added in. Next month, the bank calculates interest on that slightly larger amount of principal. The interest rate stays the same, but the actual interest payment grows each month. It's not a big increase, but it adds up. The longer you leave the principal in the account, the bigger the monthly interest payments grow.

Unfortunately, savings account interest rates seldom keep pace with the inflation rate. This means that even as your savings grow because of interest earned, the actual purchasing power or value of that money diminishes because the inflation rate is higher than the interest rate. Banks stay ahead of the game by keeping their interest rates lower than the inflation rate. Smart savers shop around to find the banks or credit unions offering the highest savings rates.

INVEST WISELY

nvesting is all about putting money to work. Unlike savings, where your money is safely deposited in a bank and regularly earning an agreed-upon amount of interest, investments are more risky. The return on the investment is not guaranteed, and you can easily lose some or all of the money you put in. But you may also earn far more than you ever could in a savings account.

Investing isn't gambling, however. Gamblers take huge risks in the hopes of huge rewards and often end up with huge losses. Investors, on the other hand, work to reduce risk and invest in things that give all the appearance of being a "sure thing." They research companies, analyze their profits and losses, and try to determine how well a business is run and what its future prospects are before investing in its stock. In general, they make educated guesses and high percentage decisions. They do not go "all in" on a desperate, get-rich-quick roll of the dice.

TYPICAL INVESTMENTS

Bonds are basically loans to a company, agency, or government. They're also known as securities. When someone buys a bond, the seller promises to pay the money back (redeem the bond) after a certain period of time, plus interest. The return, or profit, is usually low. But bonds also have very little risk. They are often viewed as just another means of saving.

Stocks are publicly traded (bought and sold) shares in the ownership of a company. They entitle the owner to a share of the company's profits. The profits that are paid out to shareholders are called dividends. Shares in major companies are bought and sold through stock exchanges, such as the New York Stock Exchange and the American Stock Exchange. Some stocks are riskier than others.

Mutual funds are collections of stocks and bonds. Investors pool their money with other investors to pay a professional

Traders at the New York Stock Exchange and other markets buy and sell shares in all kinds of companies. Some stock investments are more risky than others.

manager, who puts together a mix of stocks and bonds to fit the group's desired risk level. Mutual fund investors may take on high-risk investments in the hopes of earning higher returns, or they may choose long-term, lower-risk investments that grow at a slow but steady rate.

Individual retirement accounts, or IRAs, are plans that let people avoid paying tax on the money they put into retirement-based savings and investment accounts. Taxes usually have to be paid when money is taken out of the IRA, but not when it goes in.

HOW TO INVEST

Minors can't buy stocks and bonds directly, but it's easy to open a custodial account with a parent's signature. Then it's time to start doing some research before any investment decisions are made. These decisions should always be made in conjunction and consultation with your parents. One place to start is the Motley Fool (www.fool.com), which offers lots of great tips, explanations, and advice for young people.

PAY YOURSELF FIRST

"Pay yourself first" is a bit of advice that's common among personal finance experts. It means that every time you receive a chunk of money, the first thing to do is put part of it into a savings or investment account. Paying yourself first removes the temptation to skip a savings or investment contribution. It also means you can't "wait and see" whether to save the money. If you wait, you will usually find a way to spend the money, and then it's lost to you forever. Instead, set aside some of the money and watch it grow.

The jagged line in this graph tracks the fluctuations in value of selected stocks over a five-year period. Graphs like these help investors decide when to buy or sell stock.

To get started, the Fool's experts suggest investing in companies you know. Do you have a favorite breakfast cereal or a favorite brand of clothes? Who makes them? Seen any great movies or TV shows lately? What studio, production company, or network created them? Stock in these companies whose products you purchase and enjoy are probably for sale.

Check to see how the company has been performing both in the stock market and in terms of its corporate operations. Determine if the company pays dividends, and check important details such as its price/earnings (P/E) ratio. That's the ratio of its current share price compared with its per-share earnings. A higher ratio means investors can expect a higher return on their investment. Check out the company's annual report and investigate its figures for profits, earnings, expenses, debt, research and development, etc. Many online sites designed for investment and finance professionals charge for access to this kind of information, but sites such as Yahoo! Finance offer a lot of this content for free.

Take plenty of time before investing in a company and purchasing any of its stock. If a company looks good, keep reading. Did its genius founder just have a heart attack? Is it about to be bought or sold by another company? Is technology about to make its featured product obsolete? Does it have cutting-edge new products in development? Are its competitors being beaten in the marketplace or are they beginning to bite into the company's market share?

Take time before selling as well as buying. It's an investment, not a get-rich-quick scheme. "Buy low and sell high" is the classic formula for success in stocks. If only it were that simple! Even the best research is no guarantee that the company and your investment in it will grow. That depends on other investors. If others think it's a good deal and buy shares, the value of the stock will rise with its price. If other investors decide not to buy, or to sell their own shares, it will go down. Don't make panicked buy-and-sell decisions based on any given day's stock market results. Instead try to chart trends and determine if an upward or downward movement beyond the short-term is likely. Then act accordingly.

KEEP SCORE

It's impossible to know how much you're saving or spending unless you keep track of your money. It's like checking the map to see where you are, where you've been, and where you're going, or checking the scoreboard at a ball game to see who's ahead.

BASIC ACCOUNTING

A couple of important terms in money scorekeeping are debit and credit. When income (deposits, dividends, interest earned) is written down in a bank statement or other financial record, it's called a credit. Expenditures (withdrawals, payments) are debits.

Debits may be written with a minus sign, like this: -$123. Or they may appear within parentheses ($123). Sometimes they are shown in red (debts and losses used to be written into ledgers in red ink, while profits were written in black; hence the terms to be "in the red," or in debt, and "in the black," or profitable).

Keeping score with bank accounts is pretty easy. Once you open an account, you should be able to check it online at any time. If

It's easy to keep track of a checking account online or on paper. The important thing is to do it regularly.

you have a checkbook, it's just a matter of filling in the blanks in the check register. It's not rocket science, but it's amazing how many people neglect to do it. Because of poor record keeping, they often write bad checks. This is when you write a check for more money than actually resides in your account. The check "bounces" back to the bank, and you pay a hefty financial penalty for insufficient funds, while your credit rating also takes a serious hit.

BUDGETING

The handiest tool for keeping score is a budget. A budget is simply a list of expected income and expenditures over a certain

A SAMPLE BUDGET

Here's how a budget might look:

MONTH: SEPTEMBER

INCOME:

Dog sitting: $30

Computer cleanups: $50

Allowance: $100

Gifts: $15

Lunch money: $120

Total income: $315

FIXED EXPENDITURES:

Savings: $31.50

Lunches: $120

Sodas: $25

Material for art class: $7

Share of gas money: $20

Total fixed expenditures: $203.50

OTHER EXPENDITURES:

Movies: $30

Snacks: $25

Video game: $50

Total other expenditures: $105

Total expenditures: $308.50

Income minus expenditures: $6.50

This is pretty close to a balanced budget, with a slight surplus. The leftover $6.50 can get carried over to next month's budget and added to the income for October. This budget includes savings. The person who drew it up decided to pay himself or herself first, setting aside 10 percent of his or her earnings. That amount, $31.50, is recorded under expenditures and subtracted along with the other expenses.

time period. It shows you exactly how much you can afford to spend. Every successful money manager draws up and sticks to a budget.

To get started, take a pencil and sheet of paper (lined paper is best) or open a worksheet in your computer's spreadsheet program. There is also specially designed finance software available for sale or free on the Web (Quicken, the Mint). Many Web sites have blank worksheets, like this one at PBS Kids: http://pbskids.org/itsmylife/money/managing/print_blank_budget_sheet.html.

However you draw it up or whatever electronic worksheet or program you use, the budget should include:

- The time period covered.
- A list of all income sources and amounts. These would include pay from a job, tips, allowance, and gifts. Each item gets listed on its own line. You could break this down into fixed income (weekly pay or allowance) and additional income (gifts, odd jobs).
- Total income.
- A list of fixed expenditures (ones you know about ahead of time and pay regularly, like monthly bills, dues, or subscriptions). There are probably certain things you buy regularly and can plan ahead for, like lunches, after-school snacks, certain magazines, MP3 downloads, or movie tickets. If you know you're going to spend money on something within the budget's given time period, it goes here, along with the amount. Each item goes on its own line.

	A	B	C	D	E
1			Emily's Monthly Budget		
2					
3		Monthly Income		Expenses	
4	allowance	$40.00			
5	babysitting	$96.00			
6					
7					
8	snacks			$40	
9	movies			$14	
10	clothes			$30	
11	savings account			$40	
12	misc. expenses			$12	
13					
14	Total	$136		$136	
15					
16					
17					
18					
19					
20					

Sheet1   Ready   Sum=$96.00   SCRL CAPS NUM

The simplest kind of budget shows income and expenditure. Others may separate fixed, or permanent, expenses from ones that aren't planned. They may also separate regular and unexpected income.

- Total fixed expenditures. Once you have this total, you subtract it from your total income. The remaining amount is what you have left for saving and/or spending on other things.
- A list of other expenditures. Any unexpected or unplanned expenses go into this section of the budget as soon as you become aware of them.
- Total expenditures. If this figure is greater than your income, you have a budget deficit, which can mean trouble. If the total expenditure figure is less than your income, you have a budget surplus. If the two figures are equal, you have a balanced budget.

BORROWER BEWARE!

When you borrow money to buy things, you are said to be buying "on credit." Credit can help pay for a lot of big-ticket purchases—a car, a home, college tuition. But if it isn't used wisely, it can also ruin your finances and your future ability to borrow money.

LOAN INTEREST

You saw how interest works for savings. You get paid a small percentage of your principal because you are in effect loaning money to the bank or other financial institution. Interest is at work when you borrow as well, only this time it doesn't work in your favor—not by a long shot. The interest rates that apply to borrowed money (such as bank loans, home mortgages, car loans, and credit cards) are always higher than savings account interest rates.

Lenders advertise their loans using the abbreviation APR, which stands for annual percentage rate. From the borrower's perspective, a lower APR is better, of course. Lower rates mean you will pay less to repay the loan than you would if the interest rate were higher. If you borrow $10,000 at an APR of 8 percent, the bank will charge you $800 dollars a year, or $66 a month, in interest until the loan is paid off. Paying that $800 does nothing to reduce the $10,000

Debt can be hazardous to your financial health. Many people struggle to pay the interest on their loans, but they never get out of debt because they can't pay off the principal.

you owe (the original loan amount, or principal). It is merely the fee charged for taking out the loan. You must pay back both the $10,000 and whatever interest accrues over the course of the loan. This is why it's better to pay off loans as quickly as possible to avoid accumulating interest charges. If you are paying off only interest and not any principal each month, the loan will never be repaid and you will be paying interest forever and not getting any further ahead.

With credit cards, which are a form of borrowing, the interest game is a disaster waiting to happen. Credit cards have huge interest rates, some well over 20 percent APR. Let's say you've run up your credit card bill to $10,000, at 20 percent APR. That means you need to come up with $2,000 a year, or $166.66 a month just to pay off the interest. Even after doing so, you'd still be stuck with the $10,000 owed on the credit card, with more interest being charged every month. The debt doesn't go away until both interest and all the principal are repaid.

The credit card company will be delighted if you make only the minimum interest payments. Credit card companies often provide a suggested or minimum payment on the credit card bill. These are designed to tempt you not to pay your bill off in full, but instead to incur interest payments. If you do as the credit card company suggests, you'll be paying $166.66 a month for

GOOD DEBT VS. BAD DEBT

Some financial planners like to distinguish between "good debt" and "bad debt." What do they mean by that? Bad debt means borrowing to spend money that you'll never see again, on things like food and entertainment. Good debt means borrowing to buy something that will help you make money or build capital and equity in the future. It's much like an investment. If you want to start a computer repair business, and you borrow to buy software and hardware, that could be viewed as good debt because the purchases are going to help you make money. Whether we look at debt as good or bad, however, it's still debt, and it still must be repaid.

the rest of your life, and you'll die still owing $10,000, despite the fact that you've already sent the credit card company tens of thousands of dollars in interest payments. In order to break this debt spiral, you should pay off your credit card bill in full every month or at least pay off part of the principal each month. And just because credit cards are easy and convenient to use, you still must stick to your resolution not to spend more than you make. Credit cards give the illusion that you can buy now and pay later, but what you are really doing is buying now and paying much, much more at a later time.

Equifax and other credit reporting bureaus keep track of our loans and repayments and score our behavior as borrowers. A bad score means future loans will be more expensive and harder to get.

YOU ARE BEING WATCHED!

From the moment you get a credit card, a school loan, or a car loan, you are being watched. Credit bureaus collect information on your debts and payments and put together a "score." These scores range from below 620 (poor) to above 720 (very good). Even the tiniest late payment or nonpayment of a bill can drop your score. Credit scores don't reflect how much money you make, just how much you borrow and how well you pay it back. Rich people can have lousy credit scores.

The big three U.S. credit bureaus are Experian, TransUnion, and Equifax. They sell your credit history and score to lenders such as banks and credit card companies. Throughout your life, every time you apply for a loan, the lender will check this credit report. Depending on the score, you might be denied a loan. Or you might get a loan, but only with a high interest rate: bad score, pay more. The same goes for credit cards. Even people with terrible credit scores can obtain a credit card, but they usually carry outrageous interest rates. In order to get the cheapest loans, you have to maintain a spotless credit history.

TIP #7

SET SPENDING PRIORITIES

No matter how much income you have, you won't get ahead by spending it. Buying stuff can be a lot of fun. And no wonder! From the moment we start watching television, we are put on a lifetime diet of commercials. When we learn to read, we get even heavier doses of product advertising from all sides— from Internet ads to candy wrappers. By the time we hit our teens, we have already survived years of commercial bombardment, and the onslaught is just beginning. By retirement, we will have seen and heard millions of messages that say basically one thing: buy this product now!

Besides the obvious print, radio, television, and Internet advertising, companies pay lots of money to get their products placed or mentioned in settings where we'll see them and like them—in movies, on TV shows, in blogs, and other media. Many top athletes and celebrities "pitch" products. They seem to have glamorous lives and glamorous stuff. It's only normal to think that if we get some of that same stuff, we get a piece of their glamour, too.

WANTING IS NOT NEEDING

Welcome to the consumer society! It's called "consumer" because that's exactly what we're supposed to do: Buy something and consume it until it's all gone, and then we must buy and consume some more. Then we're supposed to buy more of it.

Just as there's good debt and bad debt, however, there's also smart spending and dumb spending. There's spending on things we need, and spending on things we just happen to want right

Before making a big purchase, it's a good idea to do some research and compare prices. It's never fun to realize after the fact that you spent more than you needed to.

now. Sometimes it's hard to tell the difference. We can't always be sure ahead of time whether we're making a good decision. Afterward, we usually know when the shopping thrill dies down, and buyer remorse sets in.

We're either happy with the deal or wish we'd never spent the money. It's never easy to look back at our decisions and admit to ourselves that we were wrong. That kind of honesty takes courage, and not everybody has it. People who do have it are less likely to keep making similar mistakes.

AVOIDING BUYER'S REMORSE

"Think before you buy" is always a good idea, but how you think is the key. If you're obsessing about buying something, then

COMPARING PRICES ONLINE

Finding the best deals used to take hours driving around from store to store, but today it's easy. There are dozens of online price comparison services that gather data from individual retailers. Among the more popular are ShopLocal.com, NexTag.com, and BizRate.com. Comparison services can be very handy in mobile phone applications. The iOS App Store offers free downloads of Google Shopper, which lets users scan bar codes or voice search for products they want. In addition to comparing prices, the user can also check local stores to see if an item is in stock.

you're already thinking nonstop about it. It's clear that you want it, but that doesn't help you decide if it's a good deal. To do that, you need facts.

Facts come from research. Are there cheaper versions of what you want that would do just as well? Is this the absolute lowest price? Is there a better model that costs about the same? Do you know anybody who bought one? What do they think of it? What do online consumer comments indicate about the product's quality and their satisfaction with it? Taking the time to ask these questions provides a cooling-off period that may quench the fire of your consumer passion. And the answers you gather will help you make a much more informed and intelligent decision about whether to buy or not to buy.

IT PAYS TO LISTEN

rofessionals who give money advice—financial analysts, investment advisers, and other experts—are pretty well paid. Many of them make over $100,000 a year, and a few make a lot more than that. It's common for advisers to charge customers on a percentage basis. They may be put in charge of a customer's portfolio—an account containing all of the customer's invest-ments. As they help the account grow, they earn more money themselves. It would be great if everyone could hire an expert or two, but most of us have to settle for free advice wherever we can find it.

WHERE TO GET THE INSIDE STORY

Some of the best advice is right at home. It's true that some parents are notorious for saying things that teens don't want

EXPERT TIPS

The media are full of financial advice. There are finance-related Web sites, blogs, magazines, and specialty newsletters of all kinds. Every major newspaper has a financial section, usually with stock and other investment listings. Here are a few free places worth checking on the Web:

- The Motley Fool (www.fool.com) has a rich selection of accessible financial articles for teens, everything from selecting stocks to buying a car.
- Money Talks (http://moneytalks4teens.ucdavis.edu/index.cfm) publishes articles and newsletters on money topics for teens, such as banking, credit, and jobs. It also covers smart shopping for food, cars, and other items.
- Financial Calculators (http://calculators.aol.com/tools/aol/college 02/tool.fcs) help you do the math on loans, savings, stocks and bonds, credit cards, college planning, and more. They can be found on AOL's Daily Finance site.
- The Mint (http://www.themint.org/index.html) lets users practice spending, saving, using credit cards, and other activities. It can help you figure out how long it will take to become a millionaire or instruct you in how to weigh the risks and rewards of investing.
- Investopedia (http://www.investopedia.com) is written for adults, but its tutorial section is clear and straightforward, and it has a great dictionary. The Simulator section has a fantasy investment pool that gives you a starting stake of $100,000 of electronic play money. It allows you to test investment strategies without incurring any actual risk.
- MoneyRates (http://www.money-rates.com) is another professional site that surveys the best deals on savings accounts, checking accounts, CDs, credit cards, and other stuff. It also has calculators and an "Ask the Expert" feature.

to hear. And sometimes young people are equally notorious for not wanting to hear what parents say. And many people, of all ages, in all societies, are simply uncomfortable talking about personal money matters. But if parents are willing to talk, then by all means listen! Parents are usually the best sources of help with balancing a checkbook, finding a good bank, setting up a budget, getting a job, and lots of other issues.

Some people pay lots of money for financial advice. Others can have it for free. Sometimes the best advice is found at home.

Just about everybody who's ever had money has a lesson they could share about it, even if it's a negative lesson. Some of the most vivid stories come from people who got it wrong. A good consultant might be a family friend who's willing to talk about his or her mistakes. One of the most important things about asking for advice is simply the fact that you're willing to do it. When you ask for help or advice, you're acknowledging that there's stuff you don't know. It's a sign of humility, and it's a sign of responsibility. This attitude makes other people more willing to open up and share their experiences with money management, both positive and negative, and offer you the benefit of their hard-won wisdom.

10 GREAT QUESTIONS
TO ASK A PARENT, FINANCE TEACHER, OR FINANCIAL ADVISER

 1 CAN YOU SUGGEST POSSIBLE INCOME SOURCES FOR ME?

 2 CAN YOU SUGGEST POSSIBLE INVESTMENTS FOR ME?

 3 IF I GET A REGULAR JOB, DO I GET MINIMUM WAGE?

 4 HOW MUCH SAVINGS WILL I NEED TO BUY A REASONABLY PRICED CAR?

 5 HOW MUCH WILL I NEED TO MOVE INTO MY OWN APARTMENT SOMEDAY?

 6 WHERE'S THE BEST PLACE TO KEEP AND GROW MY SAVINGS?

 7 IF THE ECONOMY IS IN RECESSION, ARE MY INCOME AND SAVINGS SAFE?

 8 DO I NEED TO PAY TAXES ON MY SAVINGS AND INCOME?

 9 WHAT'S THE SMARTEST THING YOU EVER DID FINANCIALLY?

 10 WHAT'S THE WORST MONEY MANAGEMENT MISTAKE YOU'VE EVER MADE?

THINK OF MONEY AS A TOOL

For some people, money isn't a tool to be used for reaching a certain goal; it's an end in itself. That's too bad. Philosophers, writers, poets, singers, and religious and spiritual leaders have been saying it for centuries: money might help us be able to afford to do the things that make us happy, but it can't buy us happiness. As Henry Wheeler Shaw, an American writer of the 1800s, put it: "Money will buy you a pretty good dog, but it won't buy the wag of his tail."

TRUE VALUE AND TRUE WORTH

Focusing on goals—things we want to buy or do—is a great motivation to save. But is the dog, the car, or the computer really the final goal? Aren't they just other sorts of tools for getting us to the bigger, ultimate goal of happiness? When the philosopher Aristotle discussed true happiness 2,300 years ago, he concluded that it was more or less a permanent state of mind. We might call it "contentment."

The words "price" and "value" mean almost the same thing, but there's a slight difference, and it's an important one. Objects that can be bought have prices. Our savings goal might be a car, which certainly has a price. But a road trip in that car with

EVALUATING CHARITIES

It's not always easy to tell when a seemingly worthy cause is truly deserving of our financial support. Smart donors research the organizations they support before deciding to give. Why? Scammers, hustlers, and telemarketers sometimes take advantage of people's generosity, especially when natural disasters are in the news and people want to help. Even legal charities may use a lot of their donors' money on things like fund-raising, executive salaries, and nice offices, rather than on the people they're supposed to be helping.

To make sure your donation goes where it's needed, it helps to know what portion of a charity's budget is spent on administrative costs such as employee salaries, executive travel, and office space. Go on the Web to research a charity you're considering donating to. Visit a site like CharityNavigator.org for free financial evaluations of American charities. Charity Navigator tracks and reports on more than five thousand philanthropic organizations devoted to everything from operating pet shelters and putting computers in schools to combating hunger in American cities and towns and providing for refugees worldwide.

friends can result in even closer friendships and a great time that we remember forever. Those things have value, and you can't put a price on them. Isn't value the real goal of our saving?

GIVING

So money can't buy happiness, correct? Actually, sometimes it can. Money might not be able to buy happiness at the mall, but it can definitely be used to bring about happiness. How? When it's given to somebody who needs it more.

Muhammad Ali, the legendary boxer and civil rights activist, once said: "To be able to give away riches is mandatory if you wish to possess them. This is the only way that you will be truly rich." By that measure, Facebook founder Mark Zuckerberg, Bill

Some of the happiest people are those who help others, and they aren't always rich charitable donors. These students are raising money for disaster victims.

Gates of Microsoft, and investor Warren Buffet are truly rich. They donate millions of dollars a year to charity. To encourage others to do the same, they have signed a public pledge to give away most of their fortunes over the course of their lives.

Dozens of the world's richest people have also signed this pledge. Together, this group of billionaire philanthropists provide hundreds of billions of dollars a year to charities. "People wait until late in their career to give back. But why wait when there is so much to be done?" said Zuckerberg, who became one of the youngest billionaires in the world while still in his twenties.

KEEP MONEY IN PERSPECTIVE

It's important to gain perspective on money and the acquiring of material goods. Perspective means seeing things as they really are, in a way that also reveals what's truly important and what isn't. Without perspective, things can get thrown out of balance.

We've all seen something like this: a mom is shopping in a store with a three-year-old when the kid decides he wants something. First he starts yelling, "I want it!" Within seconds, he's screaming, "I want it NOW!" When the mortified mom tries to take him outside, he drops to the floor, kicking and flopping like a fish. She needs help dragging him out the door.

EMOTION VS. PERSPECTIVE

At times, there's a little bit of that bratty child in all of us. One of the first words babies learn, after "ma-ma" and "da-da," is "mine!" When strong feelings of desire, selfishness, and greed kick in, we lose all perspective.

You may have noticed that every tip in this book is about perspective in some way. Savings goals, for example, remind us that something we want in the future is more important than stuff we want now. When we set a goal, we are putting money in perspective. But what happens when we see something we really want, and we want it right now? It's easy to give in to emotion and lose perspective. The result? Unwise spending, maybe even crushing debt.

GRATITUDE PAYS DIVIDENDS

If your main goal is happiness rather than acquiring money or "stuff," there's a great shortcut to get there. It's called gratitude. Gratitude doesn't come naturally to most of us, even though we may say "thank you" dozens of times a day. Real gratitude takes practice and mindfulness.

THE BIG PICTURE

What good is a goal if you can't see it right in front of you, if it doesn't feel close enough to touch? If you're saving up to buy something, it's a good idea to find a picture of it and put the picture someplace where you'll see it every day. Life is full of temptations. Setting aside money for use in the future can be very hard when you want to buy something else right now. Since you see the temptations every day, it helps to be able to also see your higher goal every day.

When it comes to keeping our wants and needs in perspective, gratitude pays huge dividends. Here's an easy experiment: next time you say "thank you" and really mean it, check your emotions. Feel selfish? Envious? Probably not. Gratitude has a way of pushing those negative emotions out of our minds.

If you're able to practice gratitude every day, then the chase after money and possessions is usually put in perspective, and decisions come easier. You can stop obsessing about the things you don't have and start appreciating the things you do have. Gratitude is a very powerful tool, in finance and in life.

Being grateful and thinking of others are ways to balance some of the negative emotions we have about money and money management.

THINGS YOU CAN'T CONTROL

Debt has been in the news a lot lately. In 2007, the economy entered a recession, which lasted for two years. For years after the end of the recession, the economy limped along and grew very slowly. Unemployment rates remained high, hovering for a long time at or near 10 percent. Many people who had borrowed money to buy homes lost their jobs and couldn't keep up with their house payments.

Before the slowdown, or recession, lenders and money "experts" of all kinds had been recommending that people take out home loans for more money than they could actually afford. Many families who got swamped by debt and lost their homes during the recession were simply following conventional financial advice. That advice turned out to be bad. It's hard to keep perspective when things like that happen. We tend to get mad or feel helpless, and it's certainly hard to be grateful if you've lost your job or your home. Since we live in a democracy, we can elect or reject leaders who have made bad decisions and encouraged us to do so as well. We can also choose whom we listen to more carefully.

In the wake of the Great Recession of 2007–2009, Americans began paying more attention to personal finance as well as the larger movements of the global economy. In a 2011 survey conducted by the Charles Schwab financial company, a majority of teens said that the recession made them less likely to ask for things they want. Nearly two-thirds said they were grateful for what they already had. Though the recession taught us all some harsh lessons, an increased ability to feel gratitude for the lives we have—to want what we have instead of always wanting something more—is one well worth learning and taking to heart.

ACKNOWLEDGE To admit the reality of something.

CHECK REGISTER A listing of checks that have been written and for what amount.

CONSULTANT Somebody who gives advice on something he or she knows a lot about.

CREDIT BUREAU A company that tracks an individual's credit history and rating and sells the information to loan and credit providers and others entering into financial agreements with that individual.

CREDITOR Someone to whom money is owed.

CUSTODIAL ACCOUNT An investment account created by parents for a minor.

DEBTOR Someone who owes money.

EXECUTIVE Someone with leadership and decision-making authority within an organization.

EXPENDITURE Money that's spent.

FINANCIAL ANALYST An expert who studies financial data and makes recommendations regarding investments, money management, and/or the future performance of the economy.

FIXED EXPENDITURE A cost, such as rent or a loan payment, that stays the same from period to period (such as month to month).

INFLATION An increase in prices over time; a reduction in the value and purchasing power of money.

INTEREST The fee charged for the taking out of a loan, usually a percentage of the loan amount paid every month.

MOTIVATION The reason for an action; the desire to do something.

NEGOTIATION A discussion or bargaining to reach an agreement.

NOTORIOUS Well-known, usually for something bad.

PORTFOLIO A group of investments held by an individual or collective group of individuals.

PRINCIPAL The sum of money that's loaned or borrowed; interest is calculated on the principal (the loan amount).

RECESSION A decline in business activity that lasts over time; a decline in the gross national product (GNP) for two straight financial quarters (six months).

SPECIFIC Clearly or precisely defined or identified.

American Association of Individual Investors (AAII)
625 North Michigan Avenue
Chicago, IL 60611
(800) 428-2244
Web site: http://www.aaii.com
The AAII is a nonprofit organization that provides education
    for individual investors so that they can effectively
    manage their own stock portfolios.

Currency Museum
245 Sparks Street
Ottawa, ON K1A 0G9
Canada
(613) 782-8914
Web site: http://www.currencymuseum.ca
The Currency Museum of the Bank of Canada has exhibits
    on the history of money around the world, with a
    focus on Canada. It also sponsors programs for
    students. Its Web site has features on inflation and
    other topics.

Department of Finance Canada
140 O'Connor Street
19th Floor, East Tower
Ottawa, ON K1A 0G5
Canada
(613) 992-1573
Web site: http://www.fin.gc.ca
The Department of Finance Canada plans and prepares
    the budget for the Canadian government. It also

establishes rules and regulations for Canadian banks and finance institutions.

Federal Deposit Insurance Corporation (FDIC)
Public Information Center
3501 North Fairfax Drive
Arlington, VA 22226
(877) 275-3342
Web site: http://www.fdic.gov
This government agency insures bank deposits.

Federal Reserve
11 Wall Street
New York, NY 10005
(212) 656-5000
Web site: http://www.federalreserve.gov
The "Fed" is the central bank of the United States. There are twelve Federal Reserve banks in districts throughout the country, and many of them welcome visitors. The Fed holds personal finance workshops and sponsors other educational activities for teens. It has several Web sites, including http://www .federalreserveeducation.org, which is a good place to start browsing.

Investment Company Institute
National Association of U.S. Investment Companies
1401 H Street NW, Suite 1200
Washington, DC 20005
(202) 326-5800
Web site: http://www.ici.org

The Investment Company Institute is an association of U.S.
    investment companies. Its Web site includes research,
    statistics, and information about investments.

Museum of American Finance
48 Wall Street
New York, NY 10005-2903
(212) 908-4110
Web site: http://www.moaf.org
This museum presents exhibits on financial markets, scan-
    dals, banking in America, and many other topics. It
    also hosts several tours of New York's financial dis-
    trict, including one that explores the Crash of 1929
    and other stock market collapses.

National Endowment for Financial Education
5299 DTC Boulevard, Suite 1300
Greenwood Village, CO 80111
(303) 741-6333
Web site: http://www.nefe.org
This organization is a private, nonprofit, national founda-
    tion devoted to educating Americans about finance
    and improving their financial well-being. The organi-
    zation includes an educational program for high
    school students.

New York Stock Exchange (NYSE)
11 Wall Street
New York, NY 10005
(212) 656-3000
Web site: http://www.nyse.com

The NYSE is the world 's largest exchange group and offers the most diverse array of financial products and services.

U.S. Bureau of Engraving and Printing
14th and C Street SW
Washington, DC 20227
(202) 874-2330
Web site: http://www.moneyfactory.gov
This bureau offers tours of its "money factories" in Washington, D.C., and Forth Worth, Texas, where billions of dollars in paper currency are printed every year. Its Web site has interactive features and educational downloads as well as tips on how to spot counterfeit money.

U.S. Department of the Treasury
1500 Pennsylvania Avenue NW
Washington, DC 20220
(202) 622-2000
Web site: http://www.treasury.gov
Visitors may tour the historic Treasury Building in Washington or take a virtual tour at http://www .treasury.gov/about/history/Pages/Virtual-Tour.aspx. The Treasury and other agencies also produce the Web site www.mymoney.gov, which has personal money management tools and information for all ages.

U.S. Securities and Exchange Commission (SEC)
100 F Street NE
Washington, DC 20549

(202) 942-8088
Web site: http://www.sec.gov
The SEC oversees the activities of stock exchanges and
    stockbrokers. It aims to protect investors and keep the
    trading of stocks as fair and orderly as possible.

WEB SITES

Due to the changing nature of Internet links, Rosen
Publishing has developed an online list of Web sites
related to the subject of this book. This site is updated
regularly. Please use this link to access the list:

http://www.rosenlinks.com/top10/mny

Bailey, Gerry, and Felicia Law. *Common Cents: The Money in Your Pocket.* Minneapolis, MN: Compass Point Books, 2006.

Bailey, Gerry, and Felicia Law. *Get Rick Quick? Earning Money.* Minneapolis, MN: Compass Point Books, 2006.

Bailey, Gerry, and Felicia Law. *Save, Spend, Share: Using Your Money.* Minneapolis, MN: Compass Point Books, 2006.

Bailey, Gerry, and Felicia Law. *What's It All Worth? The Value of Money.* Minneapolis, MN: Compass Point Books, 2006.

Bielagus, Peter G. *Quick Cash for Teens.* New York, NY: Sterling, 2009.

Bochner, Arthur, and Rose Bochner. *The New Totally Awesome Business Book for Kids.* New York, NY: Newmarket Press, 2007.

Butler, Tamsen. *Personal Finance for Teenagers and College Students.* Ocala, FL: Atlantic, 2010.

Chatzky, Jean. *Not Your Parents' Money Book.* New York, NY: Simon & Schuster, 2010.

Deatherage, Judi. *Who Wants to Be a Millionaire?* Lexington, KY: The Clark Group, 2007.

Fradin, Dennis Brindell, and Judith Bloom Fradin. *Investing.* Tarrytown, NY: Marshall Cavendish Children's Books, 2010.

Furgang, Kathy. *How the Stock Market Works* (Real World Economics). New York, NY: Rosen Publishing, 2011.

Hall, Alvin. *Show Me the Money: How to Make Cents of Economics.* New York, NY: DK, 2008.

Hart, Joyce. *How Inflation Works* (Real World Economics). New York, NY: Rosen Publishing, 2009.

Holmberg, Joshua. *The Teen's Guide to Personal Finance: Basic Concepts in Personal Finance That Every Teen Should Know*. Bloomington, IN: iUniverse, 2008.

Karlitz, Gail, and Debbie Honig. *Growing Money: A Complete Investing Guide for Kids*. New York, NY: Price Stern Sloan, 2010.

Krantz, Matt. *Investing Online for Dummies*. Hoboken, NJ: Wiley Publishing, 2008.

Linde, Barbara M. *Managing Your Money*. New York, NY: Rosen Publishing, 2007.

Minden, Celia. *Investing: Making Your Money Work for You*. Ann Arbor, MI: Cherry Lake Publishing, 2007.

Mladjenovic, Paul. *Stock Investing for Dummies*. Hoboken, NJ: Wiley Publishing, 2009.

Morrison, Jessica. *Investing*. New York, NY: Weigl Publishers, 2009.

Orman, Suze. *The Money Book for the Young, Fabulous, and Broke*. New York, NY: Riverhead Trade, 2007.

Orr, Tamra. *A Kid's Guide to Earning Money*. Hockessin, DE: Mitchell Lane, 2008.

Orr, Tamra. *A Kid's Guide to Stock Market Investing*. Hockessin, DE: Mitchell Lane, 2008.

Tyson, Eric. *Investing for Dummies*. 5th ed. Hoboken, NJ: Wiley Publishing, 2008.

BIBLIOGRAPHY

ABA Education Foundation. "Three Steps to Begin Saving."
   2009. Retrieved September 2011 (http://www.
   aba.com/ABAEF/SavingSteps.html).

Benson, Dan. *12 Stupid Mistakes People Make with Their
   Money*. Nashville, TN: W Publishing, 2002.

Bodnar, Janet. "How to Teach Money Management to
   Kids." Kiplinger.com, April 2, 2010. Retrieved
   September 2011 (http://www.kiplinger.com/columns/
   drt/archive/how-to-teach-money-management-to-
   kids.html).

Business Wire. "Charles Schwab's 2011 Teens & Money
   Survey Sheds Light on New 'Recession Generation.'"
   May 24, 2011. Retrieved September 2011
   (http://www.businesswire.com/news/schwab/
   20110524005184/en).

Butler, Tamsen. *Personal Finance for Teenagers and College
   Students*. Ocala, FL: Atlantic Publishing, 2010.

Connell, Shaun. "3 Disadvantages to Buying Gold."
   InvestingSchool.com. Retrieved October 2011
   (http://investing-school.com/lessons/3-disadvantages-
   to-buying-gold).

FDIC Consumer News. "Summer 2006—Start Smart:
   Money Management for Teens." March 31, 2008.
   Retrieved September 2011 (http://www.fdic.gov/
   consumers/consumer/news/cnsum06.index.html).

Larson, Heather. "9 Ways to Teach Your Kids to Save."
   SavingsAccounts.com, June 13, 2011. Retrieved
   September 2011 (http://www.savingsaccounts.
   com/money/how-to-save/9-ways-to-teach-your-kids-
   to-save.html).

MoneyInstructor.com. "Ways for Kids to Make Money." Retrieved September 2011 (http://www.money instructor.com/art/waysforkids.asp).

Morrison, Kimberly Rios, and Camille S. Johnson. "When What You Have Is Who You Are: Self-Uncertainty Leads Individualists to See Themselves in Their Possessions." Sage Journals Online, 2011. Retrieved October 2011 (http://psp.sagepub.com/content/ 37/5/639.abstract).

Parent Teacher Association. "Money Management for Kids." Retrieved October 2011 (http://www.pta. org/money_management_for_kids.htm).

Schroeder, Stan. "Mark Zuckerberg to Donate Most of His Wealth to Charity." Mashable.com, December 9, 2010. Retrieved September 2011 (http://mashable. com/2010/12/09/mark-zuckerberg).

Self, Jonathan. "Ten of the Best ... Money Tips for Teenagers." *Guardian*, November 22, 2007. Retrieved September 2011 (http://www.guardian. co.uk/money/2007/nov/22/personalfinancenews).

Tucker, Sheryl Hilliard. *The New Money Book of Personal Finance*. New York, NY: Warner Books, 2002.

Waldrop, Sharon Anne. "4 Finance Experts—and Parents—Talk Teens and Money." CreditCards.com. Retrieved October 2011 (http://www.creditcards. com/credit-card-news/financial-experts-advice-teens-1279.php).

Winget, Larry. *You're Broke Because You Want to Be: How to Stop Getting By and Start Getting Ahead*. New York, NY: Gotham Books, 2008.

INDEX

ABOUT THE AUTHOR

Larry Gerber began earning his own money at age eleven by mowing neighbors' lawns. He financed most of his college education by working at several jobs. He began saving for retirement at age thirty-three and has worked most of his life as a writer and editor.

PHOTO CREDITS

Cover istockphoto.com/Edward Bock; pp. 5, 14 Brand X/Thinkstock; pp. 9, 29, 49 © David Young-Wolff/PhotoEdit; p. 17 © Bill Aron/PhotoEdit; p. 21 © AP Images; p. 23 © Ian Dagnall/Alamy; p. 26 © Clayton Sharrard/PhotoEdit; p. 31 © Photononstop/SuperStock; p. 33 © NetPhotos/Alamy; p. 36 Tony Avelar/Bloomberg/Getty Images; p. 41 Jupiterimages/Comstock/Thinkstock; p. 45 © Rod Veal/The Orange County Register/ZUMAPRESS.com; interior background graphic, back cover phyZick/Shutterstock.com.

Designer: Nicole Russo; Photo Researcher: Amy Feinberg